An Assembly of Myths & Memories
by The Melancholic Raconteurs

Edited by Hannah Ross
Typesetting and beyond by John Kirkbride

SRC
Bede Sixth Form
Billingham

First published in paperback in 2014
by Sixth Element Publishing
on behalf of SRC Bede Sixth Form Billingham

Sixth Element Publishing
Arthur Robinson House
13-14 The Green
Billingham TS23 1EU
Tel: 01642 360253
www.6e.net

© SRC Bede Sixth Form Billingham 2014

ISBN 978-1-908299-66-6

British Library Cataloguing in Publication Data. A catalogue record for this book is available from the British Library.

All rights reserved. No part of this publication may be reproduced, stored in a retrieval system or transmitted, in any form or by any means, electronic, mechanical, photocopying, recording and/or otherwise without the prior written permission of the publishers. This book may not be lent, resold, hired out or disposed of by way of trade in any form, binding or cover other than in which it is published without the prior written consent of the publishers.

The individual authors assert the moral right to be identified as the authors of this work.

Printed in Great Britain.

Cover art by Laura Lonsdale

CONTENTS

Memories Last a Lifetime *by Rebecca Fitzgerald* 1
A Number *by Tiffany Duffy* 2
What Lies Beneath? *by Samantha Gilbert* 4
Fallen *by Hitham Hassan* 5
The Philippines *by Lauriane Povey* 8
Amber Everest *by Becky Routh-Sample* 9
Ever Changing Technology *by Rebecca Fitzgerald* 12
Degree of Sentiment *by Becky Routh-Sample* 14
Mr Jones *by Dylan Nicholson* 15
Survivor *by Hitham Hassan* 16
The Destruction of Théâtre de la Dramaturgie *by Carma Marsay* 18
Cold *by Hitham Hassan* 20
To Lucia *by Carma Marsay* 21
An Angel in Hell *by Roksana Rozak* 22
Constrictions of New York *by Lily Hamilton* 25
Grey *by Hitham Hassan* 26
Mica & the Dragon *by Matthew O'Donnell* 28
Star Encrusted Sky *by Becky Routh-Sample* 29
Indonesia *by Lauriane Povey* 30
The Empty Chair *by Rebecca Fitzgerald* 31
Titan *by Hitham Hassan* 32
Running *by Lauriane Povey* 34
The Piano Won't Play *by Rebecca Fitzgerald* 35
What's mine is yours... *by Matthew O'Donnell* 36
Smiley Jack *by Lily Hamilton* 38
Stars *by Holly Brown* 40
Dandelions *by Becky Routh-Sample* 41
Why Me? *by Rebecca Fitzgerald* 42
The Final Page *by Lily Hamilton* 43

Foreword

A new wave of highly talented authors and poets has hit Bede Sixth Form College and we would like you to join us as we look through some of the best material we have to offer.

We like to think of ourselves as the Melancholic Raconteurs.

Whether you like poetry or short stories, sombre or romantic, this book offers everything to meet any taste. This is because we want you, the reader, to enjoy every minute of this book and feel enlightened by the wonders that await you on each and every page.

Memories Last a Lifetime
by Rebecca Fitzgerald

Looking back through the family photographs
Oh how the time has flown
Snap-shot images which now make us laugh
Seem so long ago

The variety of images is vast
The visibility sometimes unclear
But photographs have a meaning which lasts
Making special moments last forever

School, weddings, family and friends
A matter of endless possibility
Trying your hardest not to block the lens
In order to achieve the highest quality

Memories last a lifetime
When the image is captured accurately
For memories last a lifetime
Just you wait and see

A Number
by Tiffany Duffy

A number. Some people don't have one, but most people do. Mine was four digits long, and it had been all of my life. That's why I dreamed of going away from my home town. I wanted to see my number go down. Every single day I seemed to walk past cute couples with blank hands. Blank hands without the black mark that meant loneliness. Because that's what people saw them as. You were alone. And the more black people could see, the more alone you were.

So as soon as I could, I moved. The numbers didn't tell you which direction you had to go in, but I'd been paying attention to the way in which the numbers moved up and down my whole life, so I knew I had to go west. So as soon as I could, I took a plane to America, choosing to live with my cousin. The falling numbers made me feel happy through the whole of the plane journey. I didn't get any sleep that flight. But I did when I landed, falling asleep and dreaming about my future blank hand. The hand of a soul mate.

The first day in America and I tried walking in different directions around the town. My cousin pitied me, having already cleared her hand, and just walked with me until I finally decided that I had to go further down south. "You'll be looking for a long time," she told me, "and you're not supposed to go looking." But she gave me some money and the old car she didn't want and let me go. Part of me knew she just wanted rid of this pitiful person she happened to be related to.

The further south I went, the closer I got. Then I was in double digits. That was when I stopped in a motel somewhere near Austin, Texas. The double digits excited me greatly, but I was out of sleep, and had let myself go in my travels. I had to take a few days to sort myself out, to make myself presentable for my future soul mate. Who would they be? What would they be? How would we meet exactly? The questions bothered me too much and I broke free from my motel room and paid, setting off in the borrowed car and watching the number slowly creep down.

A number. Everyone was born with one. Some were larger than others. But one day it would not be there, and on that day you had met your spouse. Finally, after nineteen years of looking at the black mark, I looked down again almost sadly at my one last digit. I looked back up at the building before me – a coffee shop of all places – and smiled at a man in there. I was sure he'd realised. Sure that he'd noticed the connection between the changing numbers on his hand and this stranger stood in the window of the coffee shop. When he stood, I made the decision to meet him halfway. He pulled me into a hug and I felt him doing the same thing behind my back that I was doing behind his, and that was looking at the clear skin. We pulled apart from each other and sighed. "Hi," I smiled, "I'm Francis."

What Lies Beneath?
by Samantha Gilbert

I woke up in the middle of the forest and took in my surroundings; it all seemed eerily familiar like I had been here before. The sky was a dark grey as storm clouds rolled in, there was no indication of the time and I remembered nothing of my life previously. The trees surrounding me were barren and snow covered any and all tracks that would help me escape from this desolate place. It seemed impossible to find any indication of life here. Despite having been laid in the snow and having little protection from the elements, I felt neither cold or scared; I felt strangely safe. I climbed to my feet and began to walk in what I felt was the correct way to civilisation. My bare feet did not feel the snow beneath them as I made my way out of the forest.

The sky had gotten much darker since I had begun my journey, my sense of safety had long abandoned me and I became nothing more than a lost child in a seemingly never ending forest. The blizzard had begun again shortly after I woke, making it difficult for me to see anything around me. My disorientation became more problematic when I came across an open road. Without my sight, I continued to wander forward unable to see where it was I was heading. Bright lights shone in my eyes blinding me further and loud screeching of tyres breaking hard on gravel deafened me.

I woke up on the side of the road and took in my surroundings; it all seemed eerily familiar like I had been here before. The sun was out but the forest was barren and confusing, the trees seemed to be burnt and long dead, the snow beneath my feet didn't make me cold but I felt like I had indeed been here before with no memory how or when. Despite the feeling of safety I felt within the woods, I felt the urge to find help. Perhaps they could help me remember what happened to me.

But something in the back of my mind told me that all the help I needed was beneath me. The forest floor had been disturbed recently so I got onto my knees and began to dig with my hands. After hours of endless digging, the sky had gotten dark and fear crept into my bones. My hands had grabbed hold of something. It was a hand, a hand that was identical to my own. That moment I realised that I had found my own body; I had sudden flashes of the multiple times I had woken up in this spot and searched for help only to repeat myself with no memory.

Fallen
by Hitham Hassan

Cold sweat burns my face as I leap from unconsciousness, breathing heavily. Sleep provides me with no respite. My nights are plagued. My dreams are cursed. My heart is stone. Memories stalk me.

I cast away the thin sheet that guards me from the cold of night and head to a small pillar, directly beside my bed. Upon this pillar a stained bronze jug rests beside a stained bronze cup. Water. Not wine. With shivering fingers I pour, inevitably saturating the surrounding masonry rather than the cup with liquid.

The pale white moonlight traces through the silk curtains, gently fluttering in the light night breeze. My room is sufficiently illuminated by it for me to find my way around. My gaze turns to the stone wall directly behind my bed. Some height above my pillow rests a plaque, wrought of impure gold. My eyes scan it with a desire to rip it from the wall. It reads:

GAIUS MAXIMUS ANTARES

CENTURIO

CENTURIA V

COHORTEM II

LEGIO XX, VALERIA VICTRIX

CONQUESTU BRITANNIÆ

Now it floods back to me. The day we set off from the ports of conquered France. Eager to arrive at the shores of the fabled British Isles. The steel tips of our spears sharp, our bronze short-swords gleaming in the morning sun. We would fight for the empire, kill for the empire and die for the empire. My then heart of flesh pounded with exhilaration as I rounded up my century, my men, and stirred them into the fighting mood with a series of speeches and battle-roars.

I head out to the balcony. The silk curtains gently caress my skin as I pass through them. The stars are suspended in the sky, inanimate while I look their way. I no longer find the solace I used to in their enigmatic form. As a child I would sit and name them with my father every night that they showed themselves. A tear slips out from my eye and hits the floor. Now… when I see the stars… I only think of the children whose fathers I stole back in the days of the conquest.

The Britons were ready for us. Barely an hour after my century's galleon had hit the coarse shores of Rutupiæ, they were onto us. Descending like the wrath of the Roman Gods they worshipped not, a thousand, a hundred thousand, a thousand thousand, as many thousands as the mind of man comprehends, savages stormed our legion. This was it, this was war.

My troops were trained and I had lived for this very moment. We locked shields with the swiftness of a scorpion spearing its prey with its sting. I remember yelling, without so much as a second to breathe, at our javelin-wielders. The first wave of Britons never made it down the hill, decimated by the might of my century.

The stench of raw meat wafts past my nose as I stare out into the city. The butcher always opens early, and I'm always the first to know about it. It is of no concern to me, I no longer eat meat.

Wave after wave, the persistent Britons unleashed their savagery upon us. But we were *Roman*. We were a machine. When my archers had exhausted their supply of arrows and our last javelin was buried in the corpse of an enemy soldier, we drew our swords and charged, the sun's heat searing through our bronze armour. The warm air carried the putrid odour of rotting flesh past each of us, the coppery tang of spilt blood forcing us to grimace as we went about our slaughter.

I killed one man that day. I'll never forget. The bearded brute charged at me stark naked bar a rag tied around his loin. In his arms a staff made of deep brown wood. He never stood a chance. I remember burying my sword in the man's exposed chest, with both hands for the added force. I watched as the life drained from his eyes, though to this day I couldn't tell you what their colour was. He fell momentarily after and with him I fell too.

I watched and smelled and heard the rest of the battle, unarmed, standing in the middle of hell. I didn't think it would affect me, but you have to see it to know for sure. The horrors of war, whatever any other veteran tells you, are indescribable. I still don't know what I thought as I stood, exposed, among the slaughter. For on that day I lost all thought. I lost all emotion. I traded my heart of flesh for one of stone.

We had no right to Britain. Just like we had no right to Carthage, or Palestine, or Greece. We took the world because we wanted it. It was Rome's destiny to take the world. Nobody else's. The Emperor was chosen by the *Gods*, the Earth was rightfully his. But it wasn't. No Gods would ever give one man that much power. No Gods would force anyone to murder and orphan and widow the people of the Earth in one man's name.

I was never the same after that day. Every night the anonymous Briton with the colourless eyes visits me in my sleep. I think every day of his mother and father. I think of his brother and sister. I think of his wife and children. And I hate myself more and more and more. I fought through the conquest, dissociating myself from emotion as I mercilessly killed in the name of Mars and Jupiter, the Gods I no longer worshipped. And with each kill on my record, I fell, further and further.

That was my final solace. I, the pawn of Rome, fell that day on the British coast. If the pawns fall and legates and generals and commanders, then that can only mean one thing. Rome will fall. It could be in one hundred years' time or a thousand. But as sure as the sun's rising in the east and setting in the west, it shall happen. I can only hope that with Rome dies the rationale that brought it to power, so that no man will ever again be forced to take up arms against another, and so that no man shall ever live the way I did.

The Philippines
by Lauriane Povey

To see an orphaned child smile amidst the devastation.
Their eyes sparkling as they see you... hope.
Their innocence is beauty among the death.
No toys or home, mothers or fathers.
Just the clothes on their backs and each other.
They survived the wind and the rain, the floods and diseases.
The hurricane will never leave them but still they laugh.
Their eyes sparkle as you give them their meagre rations,
grateful for everything you give.
They are safe and they are loved and they know the world is thinking about them.

Amber Everest
by Becky Routh-Sample

Streetlamps dotted across the city suddenly lit up as it reached night time. The inventor stared out the window, and could only compare the scene outside to a child's painting; white crayon stars shone through plum-coloured poster paint. He sat at his worktable, jaded, and remembered a snapshot from his past; a memory lodged deep in the back of his brain had scrambled out and reached his consciousness.

The dark skinned boy swung back his fishing rod and tossed the line into the river. The hook was lost in the dirty depths of the polluted water, and it would take a long time for any fish to swim by, let alone be interested in a hook without bait. Regardless, the boy would wait. His friend, the ginger haired lad running across the hill, began bellowing: 'Nova! Don't start without me!' He smiled at Nova and sat down next to him, crossing his legs on the grass.

They would spend hours like this, in the silence of the river, staring into the reflection of the orange sun. Across the way they could see the outline of the city, cluttered with telephone wires and satellites and repair shops. Climbing up the hill together was their own world, separate from the metropolis; their own amber Everest.

Their fishing trips were often to no avail, and the rusty tin buckets sat next to them may as well have filled up with dust. 'Better luck next time.' Nova smiled. A wide grin beamed back at him, as the objective of the trip was to spend time together, and that's what they had done. They leisurely strolled back to the town, rods slung behind their necks.

The town was teeming with dirt, and bubbling over with people and thoughts and ideas and the smell of spicy meats being cooked at the market. It was industrial, huffing and puffing with steam, and the only colour that could be attributed to it was a bright orange hue.

They walked home through the expanse of the town, as their homes laid across a small field on the other side. Before this field, however, was a large road. It was often of great amusement to the children of the area to run as fast as they can across, trying not to be hit by passing cars. Maybe it was born out of necessity, as no higher power seemed to take any great interest in the immense amount of speeding traffic cluttering up a very crucial road.

'Watch this,' Nova said it.

One of the inventor's friends visited him. 'So, after all that, the university offered me tenure, and as you can tell, I'm incredibly delighted,' he said, pouring some tea the inventor had set out for him. 'You know those kids are so talented, it makes me so happy to see what they come up with. *You'd* very much enjoy seeing those blueprints, I bet,' he said with obvious intonation, taking another sip of his tea and raising his eyebrow.

'No,' the inventor said, not looking up from his worktable.

'I could easily get you a teaching position; great pay, great benefits, *such* a prestigious university.'

'No'

'It's more than the money, I know. It offers a sense of fulfilment. Frankly, I think it's rather unhealthy, you cramped up here, working on all sorts of contraptions.'

Then the inventor looked up at his friend's scratchy beard and plain suit. 'Who are you, my mother?'

'Hmph,' the professor mumbled, 'fine. I'll leave you wallow in your own misery.'

There was brief silence. *He came here uninvited, and he's clearly not welcome, is he not going to leave?* thought the inventor.

'Just what are you making anyway?' the professor asked.

The funeral was on a gloomy Sunday, and nothing was bright anymore, and nothing was ever going to be. It was as if all colour was drained from the town, nothing was huffing and puffing. It was deadly quiet. 'NOVA' was spelled out in marigolds on the coffin, and the boy had never cried so much in his life. His friend was now an empty desk, an empty room, a name not answered on the register. And more than anything it was wrong to be so lonely, by that cold dark river. The boy became frustrated he never caught any fish. So he sat in his room, in silence with the window open, and built things.

It looked like a mechanical pair of wings. It was a pinnacle of steampunk engineering; new discovered metal, light as a feather, cool to the touch, fashioned into a pair of angel wings. Stretched out on his worktable, the wings had a diameter of five feet, were attached to straps, and had an internal engine that ran on energy from the wind.

'My, my! This is amazing! Just what do you intend to do with them?' asked the inventor's friend.

I'm going to fly up into the sky, the inventor thought to himself, *and I'm going to see Nova again.*

Nova was sat around the campfire they built in the small patch of woodland near their ramshackle houses. Besides the river, it was the only place of 'nature' that could be found for miles and miles. The flames of the campfire made his eyes look like they were burning with the light of a firefly.

'One day,' Nova told him, 'I want to make flying machines. I want to make it so everyone in the world can fly into the sky like birds. But not on aeroplanes; singularly. I want to make it so everyone can touch the sky, not just astronauts. If I did, we could fly together. We'll both go to a university where we study engineering, you'll make your contraptions and I'll make mine. But you'll fly with me, won't you? Promise?'

It was the first test flight. The inventor stood on the top of the building, nervous. *What if I fail?* he thought as the east wind blew his hair to the side. *No, I can't fail. I can't fail Nova.* He stopped looking at the city, and looked at the sky. It didn't end for miles and miles. Nova was out there somewhere, he could feel it. He knew he was sitting on a cloud and would see him.

The wings were attached firmly to his jumpsuit, he tightened the straps, fixed his goggles and jumped. He fell for a long time. Then, he flew.

Ever Changing Technology
by Rebecca Fitzgerald

Living in a world of capitalism
Fuelled by global consumption
Basing our lives on material goods
Disregarding the things important to us

Oblivious to the world around
Especially when a new gadget is found
Living in a world of technology
Focussing on the concept of ideology

Apple, Google, YouTube alike
Sales and usage rates spike
But what ever happened to board games for all?
Cluedo, Monopoly have seen a sharp downfall

Living our lives online, creating usernames and accounts
What is this really all about?
Receiving little interaction with the world outside
Instead of face to face interaction, we run and hide

Next time when you sit behind the computer
Do not think about the future
Think about the things that have passed
And the aspects of reality that we hope to last

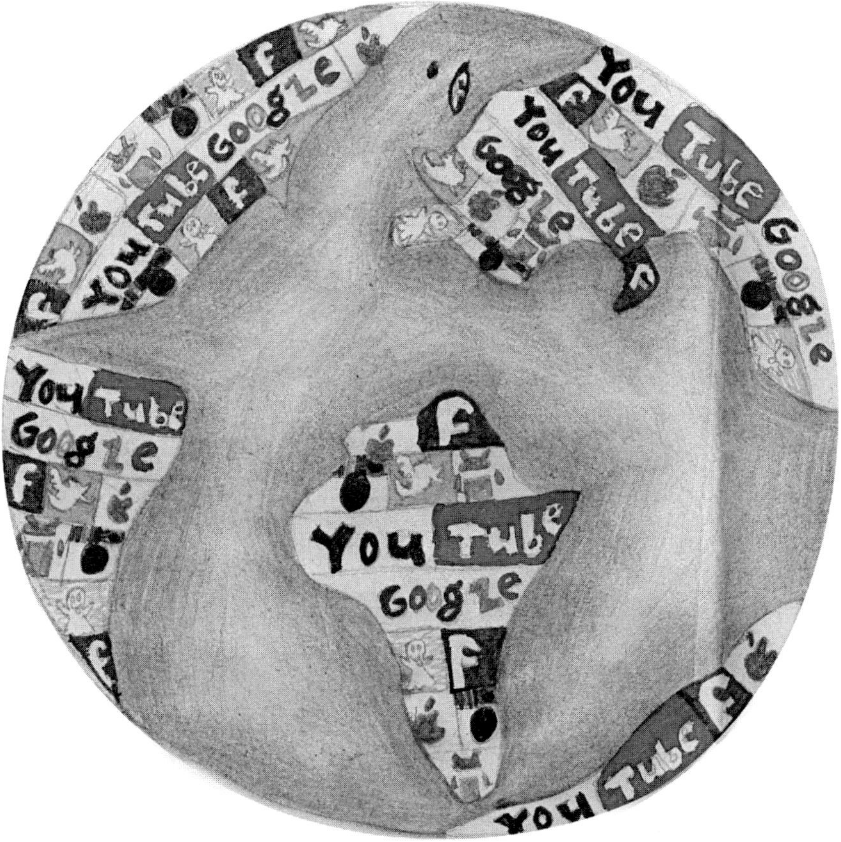
You Tube
Google
f
You Tube
Google
f
You Tube
Google
f
You Tube

Degree of Sentiment
by Becky Routh-Sample

Trailing among footsteps of trail blazers
We see acid burn in peach pink faces
Anarchy, emblazing 'free'
Softly does it, aching feet
Is it a cause worth fighting for?
Innocent die, this is not a war
That would be communist, fascist, racist
We set off explosions, momentarily faceless
We dance in streets when witches die
Secretly pray to dare to have a different life
Logical solutions thrown out the window
We have pitchforks, fences, signs and posts
With also expensive clothes
Made by starving children
But we never fight for them
We fight for ourselves
But we never fight for men
We never fight at all, we use
Degree words, degree sentiment, degree guns
With a certain degree of carelessness
Before the work we pitch up tents
With a certain degree of sentiment

Mr Jones
by Dylan Nicholson

Fred sits at his desk. The clock ticks. Time goes on. A figure appears at the door, fully in silhouette.

Voice: Mr Jones?

Fred: Hmm?

Voice: Mr Jones, are you ready?

Fred: Can I have a minute?

Voice: Make it quick!

Fred stands and looks at the clock, time ticks by. He scans the photos on the wall, posters, medals, awards. He sighs, then walks away. He turns to the window and a half turned around plaque catches the light. It reads: 'Best Journalist 1991.'

The door shuts, there is darkness.

Fred leaves, and rides the bus, lights flickering by. He holds his briefcase and sits very still.

Time passes.

Fred sits in his living room, a phone near one hand, the glare of the TV reflecting off his face. The phone rings. Fred answers.

Fred: Yeah? Yeah, yeah, I'm not doing anything, no yesterday, final pay-cheque just came through. Yeah. It's gone too fast, yeah I'm too old, yeah. No, I'll find a nurse, I'm fine. Yeah, you go, you go. I'll be fine.

Fred hangs up the phone and continues to sit still, staring beyond the television. He looks lost but his mind is set.

Survivor
by Hitham Hassan

I saw it happen.

I remember the day as though it were yesterday, but then again it wasn't a sight I was likely to forget, and it wasn't as though I'd been distracted by much in the past year. For the majority of the time, it's just been me and the big red lever at the end of the corridor.

Whenever I close my eyes, the blue Earth visits me in my dreams. The rushing clouds of white, spiralling against the deep turquoise sphere, dotted with green and orange and brown and yellow here and there. And by night, the yellow veins of light that smeared across the surface, giving our home planet a name, a place and a purpose in this merciless universe.

A half-remembered life visits me in my sleep. Half-remembered parents feeding me half-remembered breakfast before walking me to a half-remembered school along half-remembered paths. Half-remembered jobs and cars and girls and wars and bars and apples. All would appear and disappear from afore my mind's eye every night.

But then I wake and the view from the cold glass windows betray my delusions. Below me in my overlarge tin can lies a scorched Earth, blackened and browned by the last great impact event, over a year ago. Suspended in a halo of particulate rock and dust.

Why do I even bother keeping time? It doesn't matter anymore, the timekeeping methods of old were based on the cycles of the Earth, the same Earth which had served as home to seven billion people, once. They're gone now, all of them. All but those of us lucky enough to have been in space at the time.

Flashes of a burning stolen Earth play before me intermittently day by day by day. The great black shadow growing like cancer across the surface of the Earth as the worthless lump of rock loomed closer and closer until the inevitable occurred. My former home didn't go down without a fight, shattering the cosmos with an apocalyptic explosion before descending into darkness. She burned for weeks on end, the veins of light from her once populated surfaces turned to branches of fire, dying and dying.

The blast had knocked out half the computers on board the International Space Station, and damn near kicked us out of orbit. My crewmate Yuri was injured in the impact. He didn't last a week. Only Anna and I remained on board, desperately engineering oxygen replication systems and trying to grow food to survive. Why? I still could not say. After that task was completed, we set about trying to get in touch with the Russian Space Station and the Chinese one, to see if anyone other than ourselves had survived. No such luck. Anna pushed on for eight more weeks, and then I found her body propped upright in a storage cupboard.

The red lever beckons me forward. I know exactly what lies beyond and I fear it not. Stars wink at me as I peek at them through the airlock window.

In all our time strolling about the planet below, we'd come to understand the universe, even control it in certain aspects, but there were some things beyond us, some things that we could never control that couldn't be controlled. The universe sent us a reminder.

I take a deep final breath and pull the lever down.

The Destruction of Théâtre de la Dramaturgie
by Carma Marsay

Autumn in the tiny French town of Terresquille was the quietest time of year. Nothing ever happened. Nobody ever caused a fuss. Nobody ever hurt anyone else. Nobody ever created any drama. Nobody ever could have guessed that would change. But it did.

We stood in the middle of the road, Angelique and I, waiting for our cousins, in cold silence. We had our first argument earlier that evening and since then we hadn't uttered as much as a single consonant to each other, thankfully, as I'd probably lose my tongue if we had.

"You insolent weakling! How dare you question me? I've taken great pains with you Lucette and this is how you repay me? By questioning my authority now? When we are about to do the deed, you fool, I won't stand for this!" And she didn't. She started to hum, an angry and forced sharp hum that was used by mother-witches to force their enfants to remain by their sides at all times. Turns out that spell isn't just for little children.

Angelique had our mother's eyes, cat-like in shape and chocolate in colour most of the time, but the pupils transform into miniature imitations of black holes when Angelique becomes angry. She also had our father's hair, which was non-existent as both lost our families iconic bronze locks when they developed tumours that were cured by a variety of what we call "black curses" (spells and charms from the old grimoire of immoral magic) that came with the price of hair and a bit of your beauty, which our genes severely lacked in the first place. We are all born with sickly white skin and have broad bone-structures with very small heads that seem very out of place, so the added classic-witch-warts and long pointy nose and bony fingers make poor Angelique look like a close relative of Quasimodo and so I guess it would be understandable that any small thirteen year old, such as myself, would be scared of their older sister purely on looks alone.

So there I stood an inch away from Angelique's body as I looked up at the object of her hate – *Théâtre de la dramaturgie*. It was a beautiful ancient building, perhaps out of place in the surroundings of dull, red-bricked houses, taking large, geometric windows and arched doors straight from a book of gothic architecture and its structure from the Victorian ages. It was the type of art that could only have come from the most gifted of architects – it's an awful pity that after this night it will be no more. But what can I do? When Angelique makes a decision, then that decision will remain and be put into practice – no matter what.

Cold
by Hitham Hassan

The cold bites like a hound rabid from years in hell, though even it doesn't match the chill of the steel in my hand, nor the frigidity of the corpse it has just rendered. After months and months of intense planning, years of training and determination, my first victim lies before me, cold.

For a while, the room remains suspended in still silence, my mind perceiving only my own rapid breathing, steel at my side. I drown in my thoughts. I was paid to protect the man that lay before me, and right when he needed me most, I'd betrayed him. And here I was now, clutching the blunt scalpel that had ended his life.

The chill of the steel courses through me, freezing the blood in my veins. I feel every heartbeat in slow-motion, thundering through my ears, leaving only my eyes to perceive the goings on of the outside world. The whiteness of the room blinds me, obnoxious light glaring at me from all directions. I close the final connection between myself and the world.

His family are but a few metres away. How would they react, when they came upon the image of their beloved father and husband's corpse? How would they take it? How would they deal with my twisted handiwork. The realisation comes to me that I have destroyed a family. I am a murderer.

My eyes burst open and the real world begins to soak in again. My palpitating heart is suddenly drowned out by the sound of a flat, linear beep from beside me. A breath escapes my mouth and the cold scalpel falls from my limp hand, clattering against the white-tiled floor. The flat beep becomes unbearably loud. I don't know what to do, what to think or anything else.

Something warm suddenly settles on my upper arm. I am back in the real world.

"Doctor," the nurse says, her hand on my arm, "Doctor, there was nothing we could do, the injury was too grievous." She swallowed. "It's not your fault, Doctor,

You did everything you could…"

To Lucia
by Carma Marsay

To Lucia,

This is an apology. I know you said that we had hope, that I had hope. But that is a lie and you know it. How could an artist such as myself live in utter blackness? It is idiocy to think it and you are no idiot, although you feign it when it serves your purpose.

The day that I found out that I was going blind, I felt like strangling that optician. I wanted to accuse that old hag of being retarded, unable to give accurate consultation, but even I couldn't deny that I could no longer see the letters clearly. That's how it all started – the blurriness shielded my eyes from letters, from Dickinson and Keats, then it shielded my eyes from my furniture, my radio and my chairs, before that it shielded me from art, from Picasso and Gorey, and from my own work, of you, my sweetheart.

But, at least that picture remains in my memory, a picture that will never tarnish or shatter. Please understand that my departure from you was not of choice, but necessity. An artist cannot live without sight, it would be like you living without air or water – it's an impossibility. My love, please know that I am praying, even as I hang from the ceiling, that all your beliefs of heaven are true and that I will find you there, my Lucia.

Eternally yours,

Alex Agosto.

An Angel in Hell
by Roksana Rozak

My skin was burning up with the rest of hell. How could they stand this vile place? Instead of the brilliant pillars of light, I was surrounded by darkness and fire. One wrong turn was all it took. I was alone.

"I would rather die by the hand of Lucifer himself than be stranded here forever. But I know that he would not kill me, he'd torture me for all eternity." Nervous and half crazed, I muttered to myself.

There is no point in staying here, I thought, I need to keep moving. Hopefully I could avoid hell's residents, but it was a short lived fantasy as two creatures now stood before me.

"Hey, look! Is that what I think it is?"

"An angel!" The demons shrieked in delight.

I cringed and tried to back away, when another one came up behind me. I was surrounded. It would be over now. Release at last.

"A beautiful angel. So much in fact, that I will risk lord Lucifer's wrath to say she is more beautiful than him." The demon looked thoughtful. "It would be a waste to kill her, eat her, or damage that pretty face with our claws. We could tame her, I suppose."

The other two burst out laughing. "Tame an angel? You? Has your brain fried in the flames of hell?"

"We can treat her well. At first."

They advanced on me during their conversation, and I knew this would be trouble. Hurry up, hurry up and do it already! I wanted to return to my Father in heaven, and beg his forgiveness for straying to this abominable place.

The demons had other plans. They tied my arms, and my wings, and dragged me along by my hair. They chatted and laughed all the while, making crude jokes about what I could do for them in exchange for their generosity. Sparing my life was a cruel form of torture, not a favour they could collect on whenever they wished. If only I had my powers here, I would annihilate these disgusting creatures in a heartbeat.

For many weeks, I was their main party attraction. The baths in hell's fiery pits and constant absence of light had turned my pure wings black, and my hair a crimson shade of blood. My eyes too have suffered the same fate, now soulless pools filled with darkness. I could never go back like this.

I grew stronger every day. Every weakness hell presented has turned into an advantage. My powers returned, but felt different. They were darker, harsher, evil.

My captors soon found more uses for me. I now killed and tortured anyone who opposed them; or so I would lead them to believe. As I grew tired of the demons' stupidity, I pretended to act in their best interests, while caring only for mine. I disposed of any demon I could. I lost track of how many I murdered in cold blood, how many I've devoured. It no longer scared me how genuinely I enjoyed myself while cutting flesh, and drinking the life out of my preys' bodies as they died at my feet.

My name spread like wildfire all over hell. Black wings and crimson hair spelled doom for anyone who saw them. Soon, they started calling me Naomi, the Reaper Angel. I loved it all.

I had just killed another powerful demon, when the lord himself appeared before me in all of his dark glory. I was choking on his power, and it was divine. The moment I looked into his eyes was when I truly fell. Overwhelmed by fear and admiration, I knelt before him.

"Naomi." One word and I was his. I would do anything, follow him anywhere, if only to hear him say my name.

"My lord Lucifer."

He smiled, and my heart stopped. I had died and been reborn as his servant.

"Come."

I followed.

In his palace, I was given my own living quarters, armour, weaponry, food and money. All in the exchange for my service, and I served him well.

"You have become my greatest warrior, Naomi. All of hell knows your name and trembles at the sound of it. I am proud of you."

I lived for his praise; it was my salvation.

"I am honoured, my lord."

I loved his smile whenever I called him 'my lord' instead of 'Lucifer', like he always insisted.

"Call me Lucifer, Naomi."

"My lord Lucifer." I replied each time, and each time he laughed.

"You are strong, powerful, ruthless. A deadly beauty; the Reaper Angel. I wish you to be my general."

In the years that followed, I became a great commander, and a fiercer warrior. On par with Beelzebub and Astaroth, the grand Dukes of hell. They visited me often and expressed their interest, but quickly realised that there was but one in my heart; my dark lord Lucifer.

When he himself had noticed, I became his lover, and he my love.

I was happy here. This is my home, I thought. I had forgotten about the brilliant pillars of light a long time ago. But they have not forgotten me.

I felt a presence; an angel. Lost as I was before. I hurried to it, and found a woman with long blond hair and pure white wings, staring back at me with her beautiful blue eyes.

"What are you?" she asked.

"I am what you will become if you stay much longer." I drew my sword, and she backed up, frightened.

"I don't understand. Please, help me! If you were once an angel, for our Father, help me!"

Her pleas did nothing but excite me. They roused my hunger for blood and carnage, and I would have it.

"I will help you." I said.

She couldn't thank me enough.

I ran my sword through her heart, and watched the light leave her brilliant blue eyes. As I revelled in the sensation, I felt something wet slide down my cheek. I leaned in and whispered, "You're welcome."

Constrictions of New York
by Lily Hamilton

It was evening now, and the bright scatter of rays created a mosaic on the river. Polished whites and blues contrasted the green reflection of the environment. The staggeringly tall buildings were still visible in the skyline, but they didn't manage quite to touch the water. The breeze felt like breath around the wanderers nearby, the constant hustle of the people couldn't be seen from where they were but the air of acceptance still encompassed them.

In the *Greatest City in the World*, they stood tall.

Well, almost all of them. The ache of the area was little but a pressure on one man, who felt the surroundings like a suit of lead. The ever present air of solidarity created a weight which constrained, feeling his individuality moulded by a second hand creator. His seating near the river, alone, was a way to detach, not to absorb the essence like so many others.

Crumpled and twisted, his suit jacket lay on the ground, rounded hills of black material tarnishing from the landscape. His hands lay in a scrunched furl on his tucked knees, a pad of paper lying in his lap; the unknown expressions tied in his fingers, twirling the pen with aggression and hopelessness.

It has all gone wrong.

We were never meant to end up here, this daze of potential community encompassed us, to a level where we forgot everything we ever were, or ever hoped to be. Never have I known such a celebrated place to be so empty. Perceptions change quickly; especially of the beloved.

There is now not a day where I feel like a human. The light around only highlights everything that is not there - everywhere I don't feel like I am either.

I'm losing myself here, I can feel it, pulling and compacting me into a box - not even that, just nothing at all.

All this guilt, Mary, all this guilt.

Grey
by Hitham Hassan

A wave of stark wind ripped through the silent streets as I trekked my way through their labyrinthine constitution. Fortunately, the dull grey concrete maze was one that I had accumulated intimate familiarity with over the years, passing through it almost every day. Always walking. Always alone. Looking upwards, the sky was encompassed by clouds like a steel shield imprisoning me in its incessant gloom.

A small cluster of people walk past me. I recognise them, I walked past them every day. Their smiles are grey. Their conversation is shallow. They don't care. They've embraced the gloom. They bask in it and relish its uniting them. I get close, but not too close. My thoughts are my own, and I have no desire to risk sharing them.

The streets must lead to somewhere, I think to myself, as I do every day, passing through their unending form. Each fork is a dichotomy, my choice of path a decision between what feels like life or death. Going one way surely means I can never know the other. And thus, its existence is negligible.

My destination must be around the next corner, or the next, or the next. The promised light. My very motivation for continuing to pass through these infernally grey streets. The point at which my journey culminates, the point at which my perpetual voyage will have a worth assigned to it.

Maybe I missed it. Maybe I took a wrong turn some ten wrong turns ago. Maybe it'll never come. It is at this point that I realise my familiarity with this demonic entanglement of grey has disappeared, just when I thought I knew my way around. An occurrence that has become steadily infrequent over the years, but more devastating to me when it does happen. I'm now in unfamiliar territory.

You know, maybe this isn't so bad. I feel interest grow in the intricacies of this world of streets. The constant pattern in the slabs of paving, the precisely lined grey bricks that housed me in, welcomed me. As my mood lifts, I notice the steel-clouds begin to yield, letting through yellow streaks and streams of beautiful sunlight. Yeah this isn't too bad. In fact, I kind of like it here. I accept now that I may not find the promised light, the destination of my dreams, I've been walking for too long. My feet are sore and blistered. I'll set down here for a while. And rest.

The clouds yield further, the yellow light honours me. You know, I think it was worth it in the end. That little burst of sun, for all those years of grey. I hadn't set out to reach here, all those years ago, but I can settle for this. This is nice.

As the light grows in brightness, I close my eyes, and everything turns to black, once more.

Mica & the Dragon
by Matthew O'Donnell

The cave tunnel was bleak and barren. Coal dust blew up into the air with every step, creating a dark fog that impaired vision and a depressing mood in the minds of the cave's walkers: miners, lords, and more recently Mica.

Mica himself was a boy of nineteen: thin framed with wiry blond hair and a terrible beard he never found the time or effort to shave off. His kind face and bright eyes were currently obscured by the fog to any depth less than a foot. He wore common city clothing with a cloth belt, and a shiny new dirk of white steel he had no idea how to use. It would not stand to a dragon's tooth by any means, but Mica had taken it anyway: better armed than not, he reasoned.

Mica was not afraid of danger; not necessarily because he was dense, but because these things often passed him by.

The door loomed in front of him now. It was large enough that the coal fog obscured the edges, but small enough that Mica could clearly make out the white-gold nonagon symbol etched on the door to ward away the spirits of the deceased. It was a very pristine sight among the darkness: a warning as much as it was an entrance and over twice his height. He pushed against the door. Nothing happened. Firmly, with building force, he leant his body weight against the door. Nothing happened, for the same reasons as before. Eventually he resorted to the very unpristine tactic of ramming his shoulder against the bottom notch of the nonagon, until he could deftly slide through the open crack.

"You make far more noise than the elder one, you should really have learnt to be quieter," advised the Dragon.

Star Encrusted Sky
by Becky Routh-Sample

The man took a glance at the star encrusted sky, and with a sigh he pushed open the door of the tavern. He untied his indigo cloak, hung it up on the coat hanger next to the door, and turned around to see the people in high spirits, laughing, drinking and frolicking. The man wasn't one for merrymaking, he reminded himself, as he carefully made his way through the rambunctious crowd to the bar. He nodded at the barman, who nodded back. He thought about how pleasing it was to have people know you so well, as the man brought back his favourite brand of ale without a word. Then he headed out to the garden.

He clicked his fingers and the lanterns suddenly lit up the darkness. The light revealed the path to the gazebo where there seemed to be somewhat of a gathering, and he followed the path tentatively. 'Mister Moguri, Mister Moguri,' sang a child that ran towards him, 'we were waiting for you.' The music danced through the air as people spun around and twirled and ate and danced. 'That's very kind of you, but she should take part in the festivities.' He blushed and patted the child's head gratefully. 'I should probably go home to study anyway.'

'No!' said a young girl, 'we want to hear one of your stories!' All the children at the party chimed in agreement. A man with wild brown hair that was concealed by a bandanna looked at Moguri with a wicked grin. 'I know the story you should tell, the one about when you met Akai!' he bellowed.

A tall blonde woman with wide eyes slapped the wild haired man on the head. 'Leave him be!' She turned to Moguri, who had now taken a seat. 'Besides.' She knelt down by his side. 'I know the story that you should tell.' She whispered lightly in his ear, and with a nod Moguri agreed. 'Everybody sit down. This is a very interesting story indeed. It begins long ago, back when essences still existed,' At that moment, the music turned to a sudden halt and everyone at the party, adult, child and musician alike sat down in front of Moguri to hear what he had to say.

'I was just a teenager at the time.' He imagined the children thinking, 'Oh my, a hundred year old story', but knew they were too polite to say anything. 'Anyway, it's not really about me. It's about a girl named Desu.'

Indonesia
by Lauriane Povey

Children now play above the graves of their fathers.
They bathe in the river that once ran red.
Money in pockets means more than gun shots of the past.
One million bodies make the foundations of capitalist Indonesia.
One million died for Google and McDonalds.
They are the perfect pupils for new money, money that doesn't even exist.
The media weren't interested.
The world doesn't know.
This is the genocide that never existed.

The Empty Chair
by Rebecca Fitzgerald

He sits alone in a darkened room
Drowning his sorrows in a bottle of rum
An enemy of his troublesome gloom
His life has barely begun

He fails to recognise how he used to be
Haunted by his previous self
Passers by turn to offer him sympathy
A victim of his great wealth

For with this money he can't buy love
Without a soul mate to call his own
Pleading to the sky above
"True love I've never been shown"

Standing upon the Tyne Bridge
Alone and in despair
Building up the courage
Wondering if anyone would love him up there

Titan
by Hitham Hassan

They never stood a chance. Commander Ward's steel-grey eyes scanned the image of Saturn's most famous moon before him. His black leather boots gleamed in the overhead white lights as did the impeccably smooth black floor beneath him. Reflected brown light from the moon below entered through the front glass wall of the observation deck. *Weak light,* Ward thought as the meagre glow from the murky planetesimal below diminished at the hands of the superior white glow of the *Spearhead's* own lights.

The moon itself was a pitiful object, an enemy hardly worth the time and effort of the Terran Imperial Fleet. Through the misty brown swirls and clouds poked several black iron spires, dotting the surface. Some of these spires were connected, to form skeletal structures that looked circular from this vantage point among the stars. *Iron is brittle,* Ward thought as some of the black dots slowly disappeared beneath the mists, broken, dying.

"Another volley sir?" someone said from behind him. Ward scowled and looked to his left and right. He could just make out, against space's starry canvas the black outlines of some of the other vessels of the Terran Fleet. Upon hearing of the usurpers on Titan, the Terran High Command some billion kilometres away on Earth had wasted no time. The finest ships in the fleet, under command of the most decorated officers were dispatched to the solar system's outermost reaches to deal with them. Ward recognised the black outline of the *Mantis*, a destroyer armed to the teeth with every gun under the sun. To his left, the dark skeleton of the *Caesar*, a carrier with enough tanks and troops to conquer a planet. And of course there was his own ship, the *Spearhead*. The largest in the fleet with ion cannons powerful enough to blacken continents in three bursts and hangars containing more than fifty auxiliary craft, ready to strike an enemy below at a moment's notice. Thirty ships, thirty seasoned commanders and countless soldiers between them had arrived at Titan to deal with primitives. A sect of people declaring themselves independent from the Empire with no weapons worth a damn and less experience among their entire population than in one Imperial commander. Perhaps it was wrong, to execute all those who strayed away from the Empire so mercilessly, but Ward and those surrounding him had long since forgotten to differentiate between right and wrong.

I'm no politician, he mused, *only a soldier following orders.*

"One burst, quarter-power, aim for the largest circular tower. I want to see it melt before it hits the ground," Ward growled back at the officer who'd prompted him earlier, his voice steel-grey as his eyes. Within seconds, the bridge crew were momentarily blinded by a burst of blue light, momentarily showering the observation deck with its turquoise glow. The burst soared, dimming as it descended, until it struck a target, one of the black circles atop the brown clouds, disappearing in a great white flash. In perfect accordance with Ward's request, the metal girders that assumed the tower itself glowed a bright molten orange before falling beneath the clouds. The burst itself was so powerful that three surrounding, smaller towers of the circular form were also felled by the impact.

"Sir, transmission from the surface, they're surrendering and swear fealty to the emperor, long may he reign," the same officer as before stated. "What are your orders?"

Ward was suddenly reminded of a film he'd enjoyed greatly as a youth, a *Western* set in Earth's distant history. Its name escaped him but the film followed the same formula as the rest in its genre. Evilly depicted savage natives assaulted the good righteous and by far technologically-superior American cowboys who would proceed to utterly decimate said natives and still somehow hold the moral high ground. As he'd aged, Ward had learned more and more of Earth's history and how much of a lie those films had told. *Perhaps the Imperial press will make a film of this battle,* he thought, *the savage primitives who threatened our great empire, and how we so bravely defeated them.*

A laugh escaped his pursed lips. A bitter laugh. A cold laugh. Cold as steel. He doubled over before he could help himself and took a minute to regain his composure.

"Sir?" the officer questioned.

Ward turned to face his command crew, all of whom were staring at him nervously. "Send a message back," he said. "Tell them that the Empire's rules are simple. Don't desert and don't die." Ward cleared his throat and signalled to the weapons team to power up with a simple stroke of the air.

"They deserted."

Running
by Lauriane Povey

Running. My feet pounding the floor, splashes of dirty water hit my leg from puddles I run through. The wind is behind me, freedom is in the air. I am running, one foot in front of the other, pacing myself down the streets.

Running is what I do. Running is what I'm good at.

I was running the night before my wedding. The night the bomb went off.
I remember the blast that silenced the world. I remember flying. I don't remember hitting the ground.

I broke both legs and cracked six ribs. I travelled to my wedding in an ambulance. I sat in a wheelchair as I watched my beautiful bride walked toward me. It wasn't how I imagined my wedding. It wasn't what I expected but it was still the best day of my life.

I was determined to walk again.
Once I could walk, I dared myself to run.
I run for others that didn't have the precious chance I had.

I run for life.

The Piano Won't Play
by Rebecca Fitzgerald

In despair I lift my head
From the icy palms of my hands
Wiping my eyes from the tears that shed
Because I failed to meet your high demands

For you are the sun when I feel the rain
You are the lyrics to my melody
But what good is that if the piano won't play
In unison and in harmony

Sat glaring down at the floor
A victim of my own insanity
Alone again for ever more
I've become a case for charity

For you are the stars to my night sky
The postcard when I'm away
You are the wings that help me fly
But what good is that if the piano won't play

What's mine is yours...
by Matthew O'Donnell

J'skarr liked his house. It was a very pretty house, with red brick walls worn down by the billowing sand of the harsh Impi Desert. A creeping vine had died halfway up the back wall, faded into a shrivelled dry husk. This had initially confused J'skarr when he had moved in: why would somebody put such care into having a plant grow in the desert only to leave it withered and scarred? The interior had been pre-made with a lovely set of antique furniture and a thatched rug that cooled J'skarr's feet but did not trap the desert sand. All in all, J'skarr considered himself very fortunate to find the house as he had.

There had been one small problem with it, just a few weeks after J'skarr had moved in: a pair of elves had come to his door with the strange notion that the house belonged to them! J'skarr had been most offended – he clearly lived in this house as he was the one living inside it; the one who kept sand from building up in the living room; the one who went into town to refill the water tank. Nobody else would care enough to regrow the vine outside. Admittedly, J'skarr had found it particularly strange that the door had been locked when he first found his house, and also that someone had left pictures of people J'skarr did not know in his living room, for these were qualities associated with somebody's home, and this house clearly had not been, for nobody was living in it.

J'skarr however, considered himself a very generous man. He would allow the elves to live in his house with him: after all, the house was large enough for many people to live comfortably. There was even a room that contained a double bed, and a wardrobe full of clothing that fit the two elves (rather coincidentally). Yet for some unfathomable reason the couple became very angry when this was suggested: J'skarr did not pay them much heed, however. These were silly people, he decided, were too trapped in what they saw to realise what he would tell them.

So J'skarr had locked his front door on the elves, much to their dismay. For an extraordinarily long time, the elves ran about his garden pestering him; yelling about thieves and homelessness and such. J'skarr watered the plants, then decided to sort his library alphabetically; it had been such a mess when he arrived.

The couple did eventually leave, but not after breaking the dining room window by throwing a loose brick through it. This annoyed J'skarr more than anything else that had happened: that these people would demand his home and not even care for it themselves! What claim could they have over it J'skarr did not? Why would they ask for something they did not even care for?

Smiley Jack
by Lily Hamilton

SMILEY JACK

WHO DROPPED THAT PENNY... AGAIN!

Jack rumbled along the dusty grey path as the cars zoomed past. He only counted two today, one red and one green, shiny and almost silver in the moonlight. Night-time was Jack's favourite time when he was at home, especially when he read his daughter Suzy's bedtime story, but tonight it was incredibly late indeed.

At this time of night, the lampposts were shining like a second sun, similarly too bright to look straight into. They lit the path so bright Jack saw something sparkle and shimmer on the ground.

"A penny!" Jack exclaimed. "A shiny new penny for my collection. I must take it home, and show Mother and Suzy and Rover and Goldie straight away!"

He stretched out his arms, so far enough that his fingertips began to tingle and spark. He bent his back too, so much that the shadow of his body seemed to make the penny disappear!

"But wait!" Jack wondered. "The light from the lamppost isn't shining from behind me, it's in front! I'm sure I haven't gone blind as well, I can still see my fingers and toes! The light was in front of me, so that should mean…"

SMASH went a hand, right into poor old Jack's face! It pushed him back and back, all the way to the wall – OUCH!

An endless cry of words was said by this stranger. *'Sounds like he's in a funny rap battle!'* chuckled Jack silently.

The stranger seemed to get very, very angry then, but was still as quiet as a mouse! "You better not be messin' with me, give me the money. Don't you question me, mate."

"Hello stranger, did you want to take the penny too? For you shan't as my daughter Suzy would be most disappointed…"

BOOF – "OWWWWW!" goes Jack. He feels a sharp ache spreading through his tummy.

"Funny," Jack says. "Smells like pennies."

Stars
by Holly Brown

The stars are bright, bold and blinding,
but our skies are changing do you really need reminding.
Our planet is a bubble filling with gas,
we know the solution but most of us pass.
Turn off the lights, re-awaken the stars.
Say hello to Venus, Jupiter and Mars,
do it now, don't be lazy,
make our skies as fresh as a daisy.
Walk to work, take the bus.
When did life become such a rush?
Take a deep breath, count to ten.
For this perfect moment, is soon to end.

Dandelions
by Becky Routh-Sample

Running along hay bale lines
In a blessed field of broken ties
Where first love's kiss was placed upon your lips
So long ago, lips are both tied
By a deceitful spider's cobweb of lies
And the illuminescent strings tie your fingers
Bind you where his ghost still lingers
In a dew drop field of bleach pale snow
Where you once laid warm in marigolds
Now you lay frozen, soft and bleak
Rabbits inspect the pale white meat

But you remember long ago
Running along hay bales
Hand in hand
In the radiance of a blessed man
Orange eyes, peach pink lips
Kite strings tied round your fingertips
In a dew drop field of early morning glow
Skin warm in the marigolds

But now
Skin cracked in a blood red stream
Of tears, staining those once bright leaves
And it's the same for everyone you know
Who were once daisies to someone
And this is where they used to grow
You ask although you are tired,
Who's to say we're dandelions?

Who's to say we're dandelions?

Why Me?
by Rebecca Fitzgerald

The wind whistled through the trees
His footsteps crept ever nearer
Detectives search for any leads
To the whereabouts of me and my captor

The darkness clung to the air
Will anyone ever find me?
Wondering what skeletons I would find in his lair
Begging him to set me free

The blood of his victims still clinging to his knife
Would the next person be me?
Killing people, the hobby of his life
Keeping me locked in captivity

Why am I still breathing?
Why am I not dead?
Why do I hear his footsteps leaving?
Holding a gun against his head

The Final Page
by Lily Hamilton

Flight. In a word that is the feeling: of weightless freedom, yet with a destination, however unknown it may be. To finally be free of such a weight, nothing works the same, yet everything feels so incredibly natural.

Clean air sweeps through me once again - I feel alive.

I can touch and hear and see and speak; I can do everything again so clearly.

As I am writing this, it has only been a few moments since, and so I partially blame the exhilarating chemicals racing through my body for this lighter than average feeling, although I hope it will stay.

Not much is around here, as I had expected, and so I must note how the sky now looks so incredibly large, almost a hole has been torn, with all the stars racing forward to my point of vision. I've taken some respite by the tree, as with many of the events occurring here, I thought it only fitting. The lack of sound, may I add, is astonishing, what a life without the underlying buzz! No sound of bustle, no sparks of stress and fear, nothing!

From my recollection, the amount of noise produced earlier mustn't have been substantial enough to create a debate, and so I must be 'in the clear' for a certain amount of time. Of course they will find him, it will be flagged like all are, but I expect they will follow my clues down the path I have chosen. I feel that strength that they will more than faith itself, it is a fact, as I know that when you are reading this now, you are completely free.

Everything that has happened has needed to happen, and was going to happen. It was pre-written before even our first meeting. I have seen this so clearly, I have predicted the end, worked towards the goal that was laid out for me. Through this, I have understood so much, I have learnt the ways, I can see the future, and I am free.